# CONTENTS

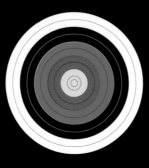
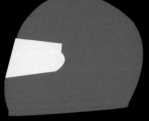

# WELCOME TO THE WORLD OF INFOGRAPHICS

Using icons, graphics and pictograms, infographics visualise data and information in a whole new way!

## SEE WHICH RACING ANIMAL IS THE FASTEST

FIND OUT HOW MANY MEDALS THE MOST SUCCESSFUL OLYMPIAN HAS WON

COMPARE THE BIGGEST WAVE EVER SURFED TO THE HEIGHT OF A BUS.

DISCOVER HOW THE WORLD LONG JUMP RECORD COMPARES TO A KANGAROO'S LEAP

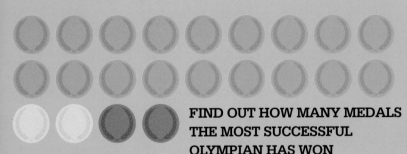

# RUNNING AND JUMPING

These intense sports push competitors to their limits. Runners compete over distances ranging from 100 metres to the 42-km-long marathon – a real test of endurance.

## FASTER AND FASTER

Over the last 100 years, the record for the men's 100 metres has decreased by more than a second. In the same period, the women's 100 metres record has decreased from 13.6 seconds to 10.49 seconds. The men's world record for the wheelchair 100 metres is 10.46 seconds.

**2009 USAIN BOLT (JAMAICA)**

**2009 TYSON GAY (USA)**

**2012 YOHAN BLAKE (JAMAICA)**

**2008 ASAFA POWELL (JAMAICA)**

**2015 JUSTIN GATLIN (USA)**

**2010 NESTA CARTER (JAMAICA)**

**1999 MAURICE GREENE (USA)**

WHITE = GOOD JUMP

RED = FOUL

**FLAGS USED BY JUDGES FOR JUMPING COMPETITIONS**

## LONG JUMP V TRIPLE JUMP

The men's long jump record is nearly the length of a school bus. For the triple jump, athletes first take a long hop, then a step, before trying to jump as far as they can. All three elements are added together to give the length of the athlete's attempt.

LONG JUMP RECORD (WOMEN'S) GALINA CHRISTYAKOVA (USSR) 1988 **7.52 m**

LONG JUMP RECORD (MEN'S) MIKE POWELL (USA) 1991 **8.95 m**

**Marathon** runners burn about 2,800 calories during a **42-km** race. In contrast, the average recommended daily intake for an adult female is just **2,000 calories.**

9.58 SECONDS

9.69 SECONDS

9.69 SECONDS

9.72 SECONDS

9.74 SECONDS

9.78 SECONDS

9.79 SECONDS

**VAULTING HIGH**
Pole vault record – Sergei Bubka (Ukraine) 1994
**6.14 m**
– HIGHER THAN A GIRAFFE

A red kangaroo bounds along in jumps that cover about 8 metres in a single leap, but some have been recorded covering 13 metres.

**13 m**

TRIPLE JUMP RECORD (WOMEN'S)
**15.50 m**
INESSA KRAVETS (UKRAINE) 1995

TRIPLE JUMP RECORD (MEN'S)
**18.29 m**
JONATHAN EDWARDS (UK) 1995

5

# LIFTING AND THROWING

Lifting and throwing competitions involve amazing feats of explosive strength. A sudden surge of power is needed to lift the heaviest weights or throw an object the farthest.

Hossein Rezazadeh (Iran) holds the combined record for the snatch (lifting a weight above the head in one movement)

## 212.5 KG

and the clean and jerk (lifting a weight above the head in two movements)

## 260 KG

with the combined weight of

## 472.5 KG

**THE SAME WEIGHT AS 6.5 ADULTS!**

## THE SNATCH

## THE CLEAN AND JERK

**23.12 m**
SHOT PUT
RANDY BARNES (USA)
20 MAY 1990

## THROWING RECORDS

The centre of an athletics arena sees athletes take part in throwing competitions using a wide range of equipment. These include the shot put, the hammer, the discus and the javelin.

## CLUB THROW

The club throw is one of four throwing events at the Summer Paralympics. Athletes compete to see who can hurl a wooden club with a metal base the farthest. The club weighs 0.5 kg.

## HAMMER

The hammer is not a hammer at all, but a heavy ball on the end of steel wire. The thrower usually spins around three to four times before releasing the hammer. It must land within a 35 degree area to record a successful throw.

METAL BASE

SAFETY CAGE

35 DEGREE AREA

THROWING CIRCLE

In 1986, the design of the javelin was altered to make throws **10 per cent shorter**. This was because athletes were starting to throw farther than many stadiums could hold – **sometimes in excess of**

# 100 METRES

**74.08 m**
DISCUS
JÜRGEN SCHULT (E GERMANY)
6 JUNE 1986

**86.74 m**
HAMMER
YURIY SEDYKH (USSR)
30 AUGUST 1986

**98.48 m**
JAVELIN
JAN ZELEZNY (CZE)
(NEW 1986 MODEL)
25 MAY 1996

**105 m**
FOOTBALL PITCH (APPROX)

# THE OLYMPICS

The Summer and Winter Olympics are held every four years. Thousands of athletes from around the world gather in the host city to take part in sports, competing to win gold, silver or bronze medals.

### THE START

The Olympic Games of ancient Greece started in 776 BCE, and continued for more than 1,000 years before ending about 393 CE. It was another 1,500 years before the Games were held again, with the start of the modern Olympics at Athens in 1896.

## THE MODERN SUMMER OLYMPICS

### ATHENS 1896
NEARLY 280 ATHLETES
FROM 12 COUNTRIES

### LONDON 2012
10,490 ATHLETES
FROM 204 COUNTRIES

## THE SUMMER PARALYMPICS

### ROME 1960
400 ATHLETES
FROM 23 COUNTRIES

### LONDON 2012
4,200 ATHLETES
FROM 160 COUNTRIES

The most successful Olympian ever is swimmer Michael Phelps who has won 22 medals.

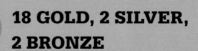

**18 GOLD, 2 SILVER, 2 BRONZE**

## OLYMPIC TORCH

CARRIED BY SOME

# 8,000

TORCH BEARERS ON A

# 70-DAY

JOURNEY FROM GREECE TO LONDON COVERING

## 13,000 KM

OR THE EQUIVALENT OF MORE THAN ONE QUARTER OF THE WAY AROUND THE WORLD

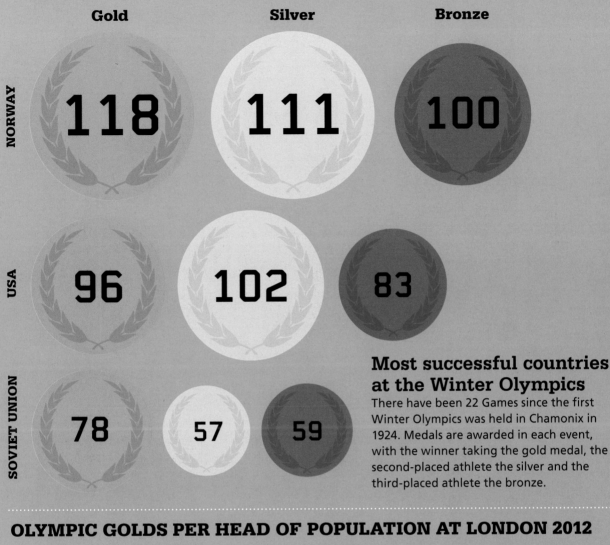

| | Gold | Silver | Bronze |
|---|---|---|---|
| **NORWAY** | 118 | 111 | 100 |
| **USA** | 96 | 102 | 83 |
| **SOVIET UNION** | 78 | 57 | 59 |

## Most successful countries at the Winter Olympics

There have been 22 Games since the first Winter Olympics was held in Chamonix in 1924. Medals are awarded in each event, with the winner taking the gold medal, the second-placed athlete the silver and the third-placed athlete the bronze.

# OLYMPIC GOLDS PER HEAD OF POPULATION AT LONDON 2012

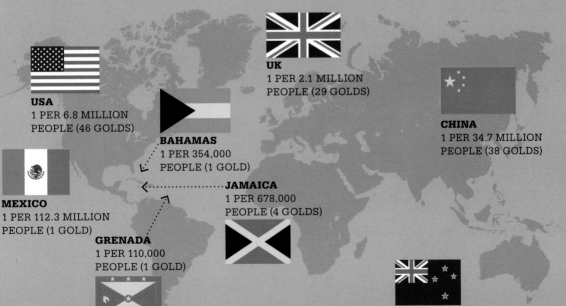

**USA**
1 PER 6.8 MILLION PEOPLE (46 GOLDS)

**UK**
1 PER 2.1 MILLION PEOPLE (29 GOLDS)

**CHINA**
1 PER 34.7 MILLION PEOPLE (38 GOLDS)

**BAHAMAS**
1 PER 354,000 PEOPLE (1 GOLD)

**MEXICO**
1 PER 112.3 MILLION PEOPLE (1 GOLD)

**JAMAICA**
1 PER 678,000 PEOPLE (4 GOLDS)

**GRENADA**
1 PER 110,000 PEOPLE (1 GOLD)

**NEW ZEALAND**
1 PER 739,000 PEOPLE (6 GOLDS)

# TEAM SPORTS

The most popular sports in the world are team sports. They attract both the greatest number of players and the most spectators. Some teams are also worth huge sums of money.

## NUMBER OF PLAYERS ON THE PITCH

**WHEELCHAIR BASKETBALL**
5

**FOOTBALL**
11

**AMERICAN FOOTBALL**
11

**RUGBY LEAGUE**
13

**RUGBY UNION**
15

**AUSSIE RULES**
18

## 250 MILLION

The number of people playing football around the world. There are also an estimated

## 3.5 BILLION

football fans, making it the planet's most popular sport

## SCRUM V SCRIMMAGE

How teams line up to re-start a game

DEFENCE

OFFENCE

RUGBY UNION

AMERICAN FOOTBALL

## HIGHEST SCORE IN INTERNATIONAL FOOTBALL

**0**
American Samoa

**31**
Australia

# LONGEST FIELD GOAL IN AMERICAN FOOTBALL

## THE NFL
## 64 YDS
**Matt Prater**
Denver Broncos 2013
**David Akers**
San Francisco 49ers 2012
**Sebastian Janikowski**
Oakland Raiders 1998
**Jason Elam**
Denver Broncos 1998
**Tom Dempsey**
New Orleans Saints 1970

## ALL-TIME
## 69 YDS
**Ove Johansson**
who made a 69 yard field goal while at Abilene Christian University in 1976.

120 YARDS
LONG

53.3 YARDS
WIDE

## Most International Championships Won by Football Teams

**EUROPEAN CHAMPIONSHIPS**
GERMANY AND SPAIN 3, FRANCE 2

**WORLD CUP**
BRAZIL 5, ITALY AND GERMANY 4

**COPA AMÉRICAS**
URUGUAY 15, ARGENTINA 14, BRAZIL 8

**AFRICA CUP OF NATIONS**
EGYPT 7, GHANA AND CAMEROON 4

## MOST VALUABLE SPORTS TEAMS

Real Madrid (football – Spain) – US$3.26 billion

Dallas Cowboys (American football – USA) – US$3.2 billion

New York Yankees (baseball – USA) – US$3.2 billion

Barcelona (football – Spain) – US$3.16 billion

Machester United (football – UK) – US$3.1 billion

## BASKETBALL
The Chicago Bulls hold the record for the most wins in a season with 72 wins (10 losses) in 1995–1996. The record for the most losses in a season is held by the Philadelphia 76ers with 73 losses (9 wins) in 1972–1973.

# BATS AND BALLS

In these sports, the players have to try and hit a ball that may be travelling at more than 160 km/h – that is faster than cars are allowed to travel in most countries.

## FASTEST

**BASEBALL PITCH**

## 169.1 KM/H

**AROLDIS CHAPMAN**
CINCINNATI REDS
24 SEPTEMBER 2010

**CRICKET DELIVERY**

## 161.3 KM/H

**SHOAIB AKHTAR**
PAKISTAN
22 FEBRUARY 2003

**SEAM**
Slightly raised above the surface

**MATERIAL**
String wrapped around a core of cork, covered in leather

**CIRCUMFERENCE**
224–229 mm

**WEIGHT**
156–163 grammes

**SEAM**
Stitches two figure-of-eight pieces together

**MATERIAL**
String wrapped around a core of cork or rubber, covered in leather

**CIRCUMFERENCE**
229–235 mm

**WEIGHT**
142–149 grammes

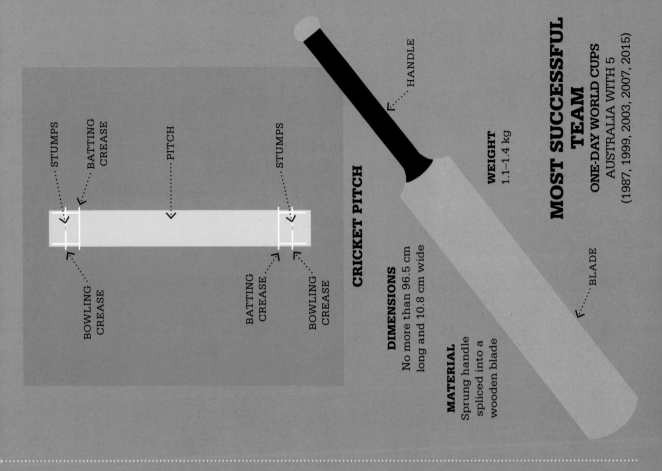

**STUMPS**

**BATTING CREASE**

**PITCH**

**STUMPS**

**BOWLING CREASE**

**BATTING CREASE**

**BOWLING CREASE**

**HANDLE**

**BLADE**

## CRICKET PITCH

**DIMENSIONS**
No more than 96.5 cm long and 10.8 cm wide

**WEIGHT**
1.1–1.4 kg

**MATERIAL**
Sprung handle spliced into a wooden blade

## MOST SUCCESSFUL TEAM
**ONE-DAY WORLD CUPS**
AUSTRALIA WITH 5
(1987, 1999, 2003, 2007, 2015)

---

**FIRST BASE**

**SECOND BASE**

**PITCHER'S PLATE**

**THIRD BASE**

**HOME PLATE**

**HANDLE**

**BARREL**

## BASEBALL DIAMOND

**DIMENSIONS**
No more than 107 cm long and 6.6 cm in diameter

**WEIGHT**
Usually no more than 0.94 kg, but there is no maximum weight

**MATERIAL**
One piece of solid wood in Major League Baseball

## MOST SUCCESSFUL TEAM
**WORLD SERIES TITLES**
NEW YORK YANKEES WITH 27

# SPORT ON WHEELS

These sports see who can go the fastest or travel the farthest. Today, the quickest wheeled vehicle can travel at more than 1,200 km/h.

**MICHAEL SCHUMACHER** GERMANY 7

**JUAN MANUEL FANGIO** ARGENTINA 5

**ALAIN PROST** FRANCE 4

## MOST FORMULA 1 CHAMPIONSHIPS

Each year, Formula 1 drivers compete to see who can win the most points over a season and win the drivers' championship. Points are awarded to drivers depending on where they finish each race, with the winner getting the most points.

## RACE FLAGS
These are used to communicate between officials and drivers

**Chequered**
Race or session has ended

**Red**
Race or session has been stopped

**Yellow**
Danger ahead

**Green**
All clear

**Black flag with orange circle**
Driver must return to the pits

**White**
Slow-moving vehicle

**Blue**
Warns drivers they are about to be lapped

**Yellow and red striped**
Slippery track ahead

**Black/White**
Warning of unsporting behaviour

**Black flag**
Driver has been disqualified

## TOP SPEEDS

The fastest motor sport is drag racing. The fastest cars use a special type of fuel, and are known as Top Fuel dragsters.

## 80 KM/H
The speed track cyclists can reach when racing around a **velodrome**.

## Racing bike facts
Velodrome racing bikes have special adaptations that make them much faster than normal bikes.

With a frame made of superlight carbon fibre, the whole bike weighs less than 7 kg.

There is only one gear, so the bike can whizz round the track as quickly as possible.

Race bikes do not have brakes – the only way to slow down is to stop pedalling.

## 114.3 CM
### HIGHEST OLLIE ON A SKATEBOARD
### BY ALDRIN GARCIA, USA, 2011

## LONG-DISTANCE CYCLING
Thomas Godwin (UK) holds the record for the greatest distance cycled in a year. In 1939, he managed 120,805 km – more than three times around the globe.

## FORMULA 1 CAR
## 380 KM/H

## TOP FUEL DRAGSTER
## 543.16 KM/H
### TONY SCHUMACHER, USA 2005

# IN THE WATER

Water sports are not all about speed. Sometimes, athletes compete to see who can perform with the most style – even when diving from heights of more than 27 metres.

## DIVING

Jumping from a 10-metre board, an Olympic diver will hit the water at about

## 50 KM/H.

## SWIMMING STROKES

Swimmers use four different strokes in competitions. These are front crawl (freestyle), back stroke, breast stroke and butterfly.

**FRONT CRAWL**

**BACK STROKE**

**BREAST STROKE**

**BUTTERFLY**

## 10 M
**PLATFORM**

## 3 M
**SPRINGBOARD**

## 1 M
**SPRINGBOARD**

# 75.2 M

Start/Finish: France

Atlantic Ocean

Pacific Ocean

Indian Ocean

## FASTEST SAILING AROUND THE WORLD

**45** DAYS
**13** HOURS
**42** MINUTES

THE FRENCH TRIMARAN
*BANQUE POPULAIRE V*
IN 2011

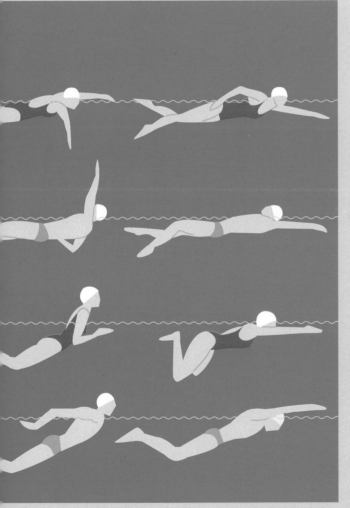

# 30 M BIGGEST WAVE SURFED

Surfed by Garrett McNamara in January 2013. That is the height of five giraffes or more than six double-decker buses.

## FARTHEST DISTANCE JUMPED WATERSKIING

BY FREDDY KRUEGER (USA) 2008.
MORE THAN 2.5 TIMES THE LENGTH
OF A BASKETBALL COURT.

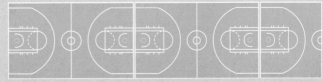

# RACKET SPORTS

With projectiles rocketing towards them at the speed of a racing car, players need quick reflexes, agility, good hand-to-eye coordination and plenty of power to succeed.

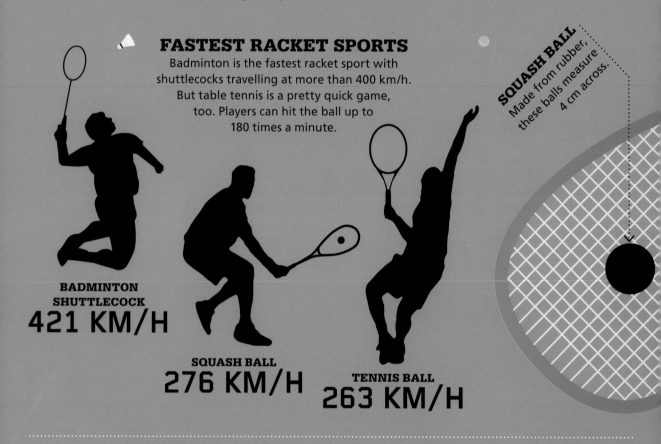

## FASTEST RACKET SPORTS

Badminton is the fastest racket sport with shuttlecocks travelling at more than 400 km/h. But table tennis is a pretty quick game, too. Players can hit the ball up to 180 times a minute.

**SQUASH BALL**
Made from rubber, these balls measure 4 cm across.

**BADMINTON SHUTTLECOCK**
## 421 KM/H

**SQUASH BALL**
## 276 KM/H

**TENNIS BALL**
## 263 KM/H

## LONGEST PROFESSIONAL TENNIS MATCH
### WIMBLEDON 2011

**JOHN ISNER** (USA) **VS** **NICOLAS MAHUT** (FRANCE)

It lasted for 11 hours, 5 minutes, spread out over three days. They played a total of 183 games and the final set was won by Isner, 70 games to 68.

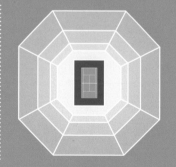

## BIGGEST TENNIS ARENAS

ARTHUR ASHE STADIUM
(New York, USA)
**23,200 seats**

O2 ARENA
(London, UK)
**17,500 seats**

INDIAN WELLS TENNIS GARDEN
(California, USA)
**16,100 seats**

**Esther Vergeer** is the most successful wheelchair tennis player of all time. She was undefeated between **2003** and **2012**, winning

# 470 matches in a row.

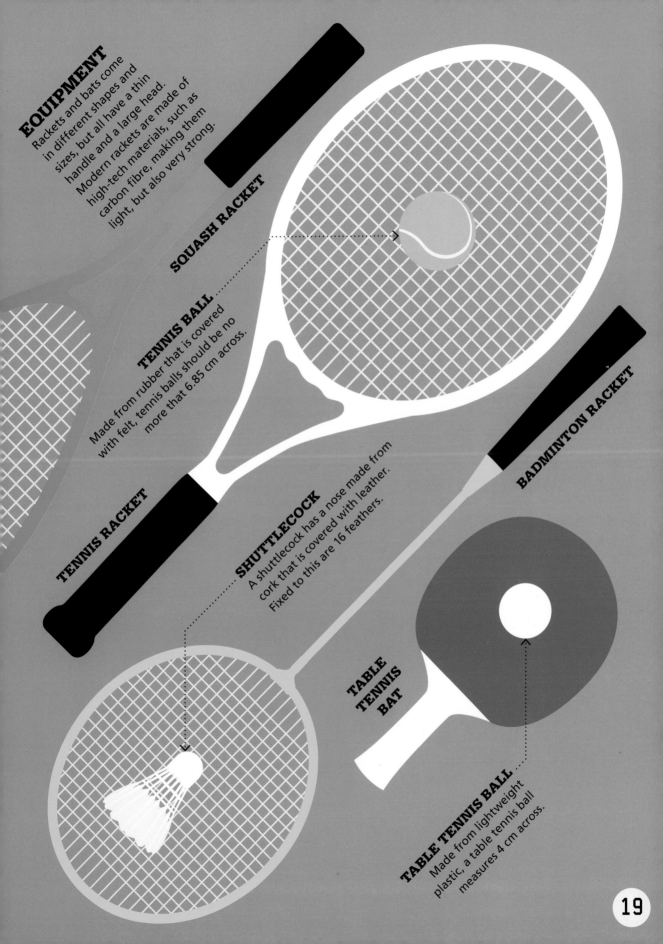

## EQUIPMENT

Rackets and bats come in different shapes and sizes, but all have a thin handle and a large head. Modern rackets are made of high-tech materials, such as carbon fibre, making them light, but also very strong.

**SQUASH RACKET**

**TENNIS BALL**
Made from rubber that is covered with felt, tennis balls should be no more that 6.85 cm across.

**TENNIS RACKET**

**BADMINTON RACKET**

**SHUTTLECOCK**
A shuttlecock has a nose made from cork that is covered with leather. Fixed to this are 16 feathers.

**TABLE TENNIS BAT**

**TABLE TENNIS BALL**
Made from lightweight plastic, a table tennis ball measures 4 cm across.

# WINTER SPORTS

The cold winter months see everything from high-speed skiers hurtling downhill to snowboarders making incredible aerial leaps more than twice the height of a double-decker bus.

## SPEED RECORDS

Speed skiers try to get down a slope as quickly as possible. They wear specially shaped helmets and skin-tight outfits, and use extra-long skis to help them travel faster.

### SKIING MEN
**251.4 KM/H**
**SIMONE ORIGONE**
(ITALY)

### NORDIC SKIING
Also known as cross-country skiing, this is one of the most physically demanding sports, using nearly 1,200 calories per hour.

### SKIING WOMEN
**242.6 KM/H**
**SANNA TIDSTRAND**
(SWEDEN)

### SNOWBOARDING
**201.9 KM/H**
**DARREN POWELL**
(AUSTRALIA)

## 9.8 M BIGGEST AIR OUT OF A HALF-PIPE
Terje Håkonsen, Norway – 9.8 m in 2007. Equivalent to the height of 5.5 adults.

# BOBSLEIGH, SKELETON AND LUGE

Individuals or teams of two or four athletes use these vehicles fitted with skates to race down an icy track.

DRIVER  PUSHERS  BRAKEMAN

## BOBSLEIGH
These come in two different sizes, for teams of two or four. Athletes start by pushing the bobsleigh along the track, before jumping in.

## FASTEST SPEED IN A BOBSLEIGH
# 143 KM/H

## TOP SPEED ON A SKELETON
# 146.4 KM/H

## SKELETON
To start, the athlete runs along the track before leaping, face down, onto the skeleton.

## LUGE
To start, the athlete sits on the luge before pulling themselves forwards with his or her hands and racing down the track.

## TOP SPEED ON A LUGE
# 139.4 KM/H

## SKI JUMPING
The longest ski jump is 251.5 metres by Anders Fannemel of Norway in 2015 – the length of nearly 2.5 football pitches.

# 251.5 M

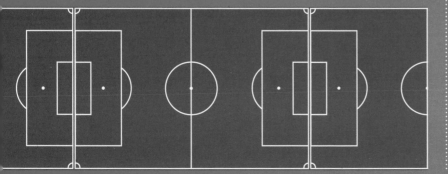

# SKATING
Skaters use different types and shapes of skate, depending on the sport they are taking part in.

TOE PICK  HIGH BOOT

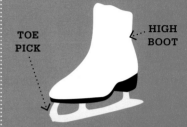

## FIGURE SKATE
These have a curved blade and a toe pick, which is used for jumps and other dance moves on the ice.

LOW BOOT

LONG BLADE

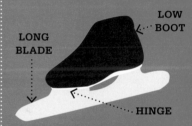

HINGE

## SPEED SKATE
The blade is connected to the boot by a hinge. They are also called clap skates, because of the sound they make while skating.

PROTECTED TOE BOX  TENDON GUARD

## ICE HOCKEY SKATE
These have flat blades and a boot that is made from moulded plastic to protect and support the feet and ankles.

# TARGET SPORTS

A good aim is the name of the game here, and for that target sports men and women need eyes like hawks, steady hands and a calm, focused attitude.

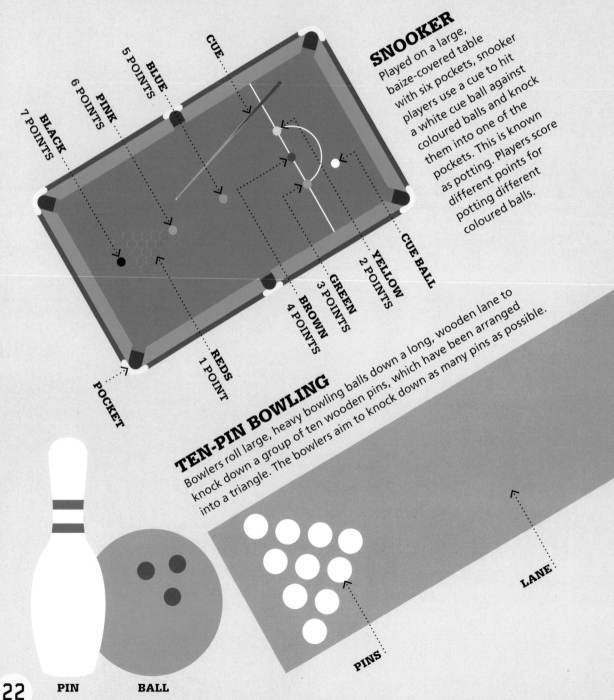

### SNOOKER

Played on a large, baize-covered table with six pockets, snooker players use a cue to hit a white cue ball against coloured balls and knock them into one of the pockets. This is known as potting. Players score different points for potting different coloured balls.

CUE

BLUE
5 POINTS

PINK
6 POINTS

BLACK
7 POINTS

YELLOW
2 POINTS

GREEN
3 POINTS

BROWN
4 POINTS

CUE BALL

REDS
1 POINT

POCKET

### TEN-PIN BOWLING

Bowlers roll large, heavy bowling balls down a long, wooden lane to knock down a group of ten wooden pins, which have been arranged into a triangle. The bowlers aim to knock down as many pins as possible.

LANE

PINS

PIN

BALL

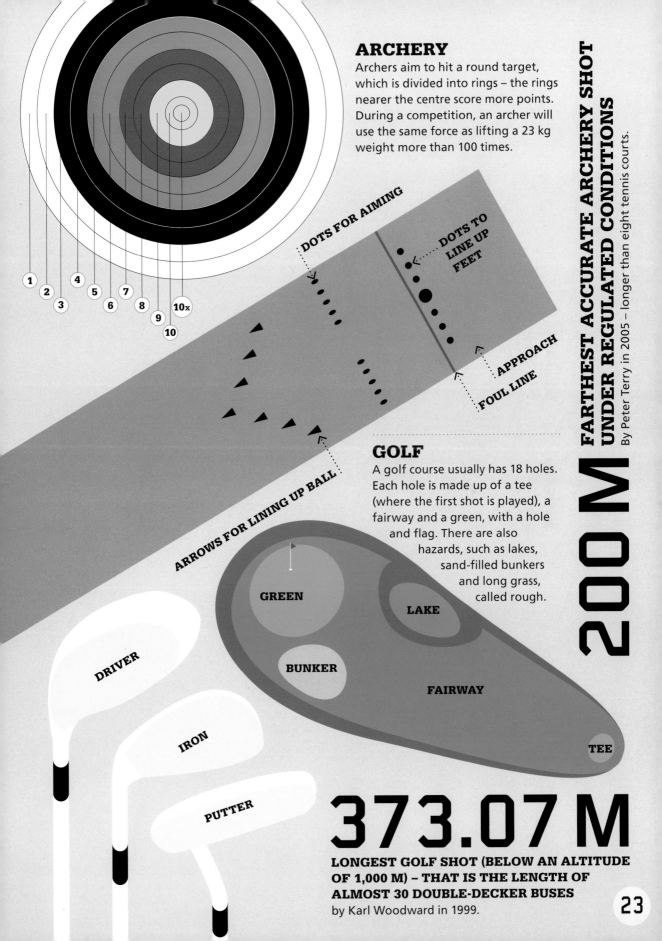

## ARCHERY

Archers aim to hit a round target, which is divided into rings – the rings nearer the centre score more points. During a competition, an archer will use the same force as lifting a 23 kg weight more than 100 times.

1
2
3
4
5
6
7
8
9
10
10x

DOTS FOR AIMING

DOTS TO LINE UP FEET

APPROACH

FOUL LINE

ARROWS FOR LINING UP BALL

FARTHEST ACCURATE ARCHERY SHOT UNDER REGULATED CONDITIONS

## 200 M

By Peter Terry in 2005 – longer than eight tennis courts.

## GOLF

A golf course usually has 18 holes. Each hole is made up of a tee (where the first shot is played), a fairway and a green, with a hole and flag. There are also hazards, such as lakes, sand-filled bunkers and long grass, called rough.

GREEN

LAKE

BUNKER

FAIRWAY

TEE

DRIVER

IRON

PUTTER

## 373.07 M

LONGEST GOLF SHOT (BELOW AN ALTITUDE OF 1,000 M) – THAT IS THE LENGTH OF ALMOST 30 DOUBLE-DECKER BUSES
by Karl Woodward in 1999.

# ANIMAL SPORTS

With the fastest greyhounds capable of running nearly twice as quickly as the quickest human, it seems that sometimes four legs really are better than two.

## HORSE RACING

Perhaps the most famous steeplechase (race over fences) is the Grand National, held at Aintree, UK. Horses and riders race over 7,242 metres and jump about 30 fences. One of the most difficult is Becher's Brook, where the landing area is much lower than the fence.

1.47 METRES

2.07 METRES

**BECHER'S BROOK**

OVER SHORT RACES (UP TO 160 KM), PIGEONS HAVE BEEN RECORDED FLYING AT SPEEDS OF NEARLY

# 180 KM/H

MAKING THEM THE FASTEST ANIMALS USED IN SPORT.

Some pigeon races are held over distances of up to 1,800 km – the equivalent of flying from London to Tangier, Morocco.

## POLO

This team sport sees groups of riders try to knock a ball through an opponent's goal using a long stick while riding an animal. It is usually played on horseback, but versions of the sport use camels and even elephants.

**Endurance** horse races cover about **160 km** and may take riders up to **12 hours** to complete.

# 70.76 KM/H

Record race speed for a horse was 70.76 km/h. This was set by Winning Brew at the Penn National Race Course, Grantville, USA, in 2008.

FASTEST SPEED
FOR A GREYHOUND
# 72 KM/H

FASTEST SPEED
FOR A HUMAN
# 37.5 KM/H

# CROWDS AND ARENAS

Sports can be staged almost anywhere. While many are held in specially built stadiums and arenas, some, such as the Tour de France, take place along the roads of entire countries!

SEATING

FINISH LINE

Used for chariot racing, the U-shaped Circus Maximus in ancient Rome could seat a crowd of up to

# 250,000

STARTING GATES

## LARGEST CROWDS

The biggest games attract the biggest crowds. The world's largest sporting venue, the Indianapolis Motor Speedway, has seating for 257,325. But including standing spectators, it may be able to accommodate up to 400,000 people.

**FOOTBALL**
BRAZIL V PARAGUAY 1954
**MARACANÃ STADIUM, BRAZIL**
# 183,513

**BASEBALL**
LA DODGERS V BOSTON RED SOX 2008
**LOS ANGELES COLISEUM, USA**
# 115,300

ATTENDANCE FIGURES FOR CROWDS WATCHING THE ENTIRE TOUR DE FRANCE RANGE FROM

# 12–15 MILLION

# LARGEST TEAM SPORTS ARENAS TODAY

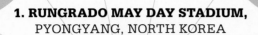

**1. RUNGRADO MAY DAY STADIUM,**
PYONGYANG, NORTH KOREA

## 150,000

**2. SALT LAKE STADIUM,**
KOLKATA, INDIA
## 120,000

**3. MICHIGAN STADIUM,**
ANN ARBOR, USA
## 109,901

**4. BEAVER STADIUM,**
PENNSYLVANIA, USA
## 106,572

**5. ESTADIO AZTECA,**
MEXICO CITY, MEXICO
## 105,064

**WEMBLEY STADIUM**

Wembley Stadium, London, was built using **23,000 tonnes** of steel. The large arch used **1,750 tonnes** of steel alone, the same mass as 10 jumbo jets.

**RUGBY UNION**
NEW ZEALAND V AUSTRALIA 2000
**STADIUM AUSTRALIA, AUSTRALIA**
## 109,874

**BASKETBALL**
NBA ALL-STAR GAME 2010
**COWBOYS STADIUM, USA**
## 108,713

**TENNIS**
KIM CLIJSTERS (BELGIUM) V SERENA WILLIAMS (USA) 2010
**KING BAUDOUIN STADIUM, BELGIUM**
## 35,681

# PRIZES AND TROPHIES

Winners of sporting competitions are usually awarded prizes. These can be cups, medals, enormous trophies and even items of clothing.

## THE BIGGEST TROPHIES

**DAVIS CUP**
(TENNIS)
**110 CM** TALL
**107 CM** IN
DIAMETER
WEIGHS **105 KG**

**STANLEY CUP**
(ICE HOCKEY)
**89.54 CM** TALL
WEIGHS **15.5 KG**

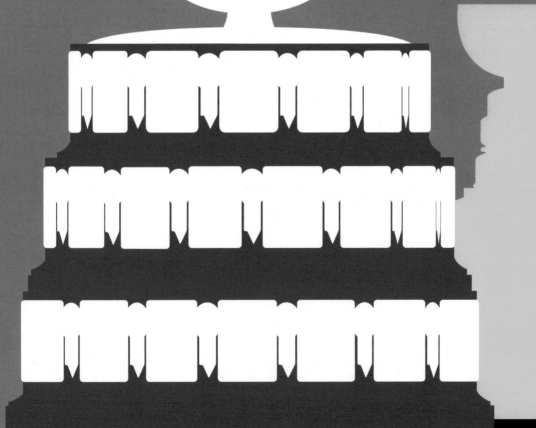

# CYCLING JERSEYS

Leading riders in cycling races wear specially coloured jerseys to show which part of the race they are winning.

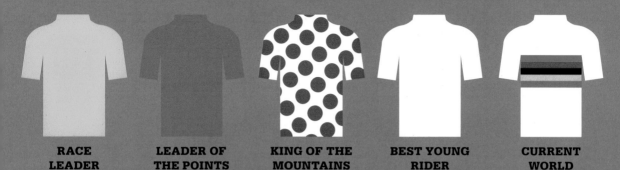

| RACE LEADER | LEADER OF THE POINTS CLASSIFICATION | KING OF THE MOUNTAINS | BEST YOUNG RIDER | CURRENT WORLD CHAMPION |

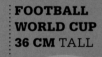

**GOLD MEDALS**

92.5% silver,
6.16% copper, 1.34% gold

**SILVER MEDALS**

92.5% silver,
7.5% copper

**BRONZE MEDALS**

97% copper, 2.5% zinc
0.5% tin

## OLYMPIC MEDALS

Winning athletes at the Olympics and Paralympics are awarded gold medals. However, very little of the medal is actually gold, with most of it being made from silver and copper.

**FOOTBALL WORLD CUP**
**36 CM** TALL

**VINCE LOMBARDI TROPHY** (AMERICAN FOOTBALL)
**56 CM** TALL

**WEBB ELLIS CUP** (RUGBY UNION)
38 CM TALL

Winners of golf's Masters Tournament are awarded a green jacket.

## THE ASHES URN

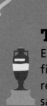

England and Australia take part in the Ashes, a series of five-day cricket test matches. The winners are given a replica of a small, 10-cm-tall urn, the original of which is said to hold the ashes of a burnt cricket bail.

# GLOSSARY

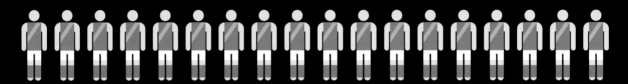

## bobsleigh
A winter sport where two or four athletes at a time race down an ice track while sitting in a bobsleigh.

## clean and jerk
A weight-lifting discipline where the athlete tries to lift the weight above his or her head in two movements.

## diamond
The diamond-shaped area around which a baseball game is played.

## half-pipe
A U-shaped channel carved through the snow. Skiers and snowboarders can use the sides of the channel to perform jumps and tricks.

## luge
A type of winter sport where athletes race down an ice track while lying face-up on a luge sled.

## marathon
A long-distance running race, where athletes compete to see who can finish a 42-km route the quickest. It is usually held on the streets of a city, rather than inside an arena.

## Nordic skiing
A form of skiing where people propel themselves along using poles and skis, rather than ski down a mountain slope.

## Olympics
A major sporting event held every four years for both summer and winter sports. Athletes from all over the world gather in a host city to take part.

## Paralympics
A major sporting event held every four years for athletes with physical disabilities and learning difficulties. It is held just after the Summer and Winter Olympics.

## pins
Ten wooden objects that are used as targets in ten-pin bowling. They are arranged in a triangle at the end of a bowling lane for bowlers to aim at.

## fairway
The corridor of short grass along a golf hole, which leads from the tee area to the green.

## pole vault

A sport in which an athlete tries to jump, or vault, over a high bar using a long, flexible pole to push up with.

## polo

A team sport where athletes ride animals or bicycles and hit a ball using long sticks in an attempt to score in the opposition goal.

## shuttlecock

The projectile used in badminton. It consists of a rubber nose with feathers attached to the back to make it fly correctly.

## skeleton

In this fast winter sport, athletes race down an ice track while lying face-down on a skeleton sled.

## snatch

A weight-lifting discipline where the athlete tries to lift the weight above his or her head in one movement.

## stadium

A large building in which sporting events are held. The largest stadiums can hold more than 100,000 people.

## top fuel

The fastest and most-powerful form of dragster racing.

## trophy

A prize given to the winners, or highest placed athletes, in a sporting competition.

## steeplechase

A form of horse racing where the horses and riders race over a course with jumps and fences.

## Websites

**MORE INFO:**
**www.olympic.org**
The official website of the Olympic movement. It contains news and information on the Summer and Winter Olympics.

**www.paralympic.org**
The official website of the Paralympic movement, offering news and information on the Summer and Winter Paralympics, as well as athletes' biographies.

**www.bbc.co.uk/sport/0/**
The sports section of the BBC website. It contains the latest sporting news as well as summaries of upcoming events and facts about different sports.

**MORE GRAPHICS:**
**www.visualinformation.info**
A website that contains a whole host of infographic material on subjects as diverse as natural history, science, sport and computer games.

**www.coolinfographics.com**
A collection of infographics and data visualisations from other online resources, magazines and newspapers.

**www.dailyinfographic.com**
A comprehensive collection of infographics on an enormous range of topics that is updated every single day!

# INDEX

# ACKNOWLEDGEMENTS

First published in paperback in 2016 by Wayland
Copyright © Wayland 2016

MIX
Paper from responsible sources
FSC
www.fsc.org
FSC® C104740

Wayland
An imprint of Hachette Children's Group
Part of Hodder & Stoughton
Carmelite House, 50 Victoria Embankment
London EC4Y 0DZ

All rights reserved.
Senior editor: Julia Adams

Produced by Tall Tree Ltd
Editors: Jon Richards and Joe Fullman
Designer: Ed Simkins
Consultant: Clive Gifford

Dewey classification: 796

ISBN: 9780750283229

10 9 8 7 6 5 4 3 2 1

Printed in China
An Hachette UK company
www.hachette.co.uk
www.hachettechildrens.co.uk

The website addresses (URLs) included in this book were valid at the time of going to press. However, because of the nature of the Internet, it is possible that some addresses may have changed, or sites may have changed or closed down, since publication. While the author and Publisher regret any inconvenience this may cause the readers, no responsibility for any such changes can be accepted by either the author or the Publisher.